THE JOY IN
Birthing
Pain

TAMMY RAÉ

The Joy in Birthing Pain

Copyright ©2020 by Tammy Raé. All rights reserved

Published by:
Purposed by Design 365
www.tammyrae.net

Manuscript Editing
Tammy Raé
Lisa Goodman-Age

Book Creation and Design
DHBonner Virtual Solutions, LLC
www.dhbonner.net

Print ISBN: 978-1-7353800-0-1

Published in the United States of America

Dedication

I would like to dedicate this book to those who have been weighed down with the controlling thoughts of their past and to those who have found it challenging to move beyond hurt and pain. Listen, press through, and rest in knowing that this space is not your permanent place. In fact, allow me to encourage you to never lose hope, to never stop trying, to keep moving, to keep fighting, and to keep believing, even if you have to start over — *Just Keep Going!*

Table of Contents

Foreword

Three sightless men were brought together to give their impressions of what they imagined an elephant resembled. The first man found his way to the front of the animal, and grasping the trunk, proclaimed, "I imagine the elephant to be like a great snake." The second man made his way to the side of the elephant's head and, pulling on its ear, stated, "I imagine the elephant to have the form of a large fan." The last man ended up at the elephant's side and opined, "I imagine this animal to be like a sturdy wall."

We can never know the entirety of another person's life. We are only privy to the parts of them that we are allowed access to, and we must make our judgments about them with this limited amount of knowledge. *Our opinions of them then are based on when and where we make contact with them.*

When I was asked to write this foreword, I pondered on what I could tell about the author. My initial idea was to relate her story to that of a phoenix, an epic tale — or so I thought. The mythological creature is driven to its demise in a spectacular fiery crash by his tormentors, only to be reborn from its own ashes, becoming an even more powerful and formidable force. *This epic tale illustrates the timeless notion of using past failures as a resurgence, to rebuild and rebrand one's self.*

Upon closer inspection, however, the tale of the phoenix, like many other myths, is less spectacular than the romanticized version. Its demise is neither spectacular nor epic nor singular — it is inevitable. All phoenixes die by fire in a nest they have prepared and are not even reborn. They emerge from the ashes as a new phoenix, destined to make the same mistakes of its predecessor until its timely and predictable demise — not Tammy's story!

Instead, I settled on the story of David and Goliath, which is more in line with my impression of the author. As told in I Samuel, David was born the youngest of eight sons and, at an early age, was relegated to the task of shepherd while his siblings were groomed for lives that were more prestigious.

Paraphrasing the story, God sent Samuel to find the next king of Israel. God directed Samuel where to go, and when Samuel came to the family of Jesse, he looked on the eldest son and thought surely, this was God's anointed one. God directed Samuel in the right way, and soon it was revealed that David — the shepherd boy out in the field with the sheep — would be the next king.

When David offers to face Goliath, his youth and inexperience in combat were questioned. David responded by informing King Saul of how his past experiences with danger had prepared him for this moment. If he could slay a lion and a bear with his bare hands, he could certainly handle this situation.

While I would love to use the romanticized tale of the phoenix, the story of David holds truer. Tammy has used her past challenges to prepare her to face her giants. Her story, her journey, plus her life, *is a testament to her faith and perseverance.*

— JOHN S. WINSLOW

* * *

I fed her, bathed her, changed her diapers, and combed her hair; I loved her. Intrinsically, I knew I was meant to be a presence in her life. We belonged together.

One day she was gone — taken with the promise of a better home and more stable life. I was now relegated to the role of half-time sister, allowed only a few daily visits. The situation was incomprehensible, separated by a few houses but living lives that were worlds apart. With her sheltered life, she was surrounded and cared for by a host of matronly women who would ensure that she had all the comforts and privileges of family life. In addition, mine was one of abuse, hunger, and enslavement.

Even though I resented the fact that my baby, my light, had been taken from me, I felt comfort in the knowledge of knowing that she was in a better situation — or so I thought.

I left the city years later, promising her that I would always visit, and one day when conditions allowed, we would be together again. Fifteen years later, we were, but the reunion was not as I expected. She was now resentful and angry. I did not understand why. It was what we had always planned. It should have been perfect, but it was not. She was hurt, and the hurt ran deep.

I now have a better understanding. We have since worked through our issues and have helped one another in our healing processes. Though not perfect, healing has strengthened our relationship, our bond, and our love. She is a powerful woman of God with an anointed mission — helping to heal the lives of broken women everywhere.

— SHERRI L. WINSLOW

Preface

How do I thank thee, [God]? There are no thanks wide or deep enough to express my gratitude, as He has demonstrated an abundance of unfailing love, grace, and mercy towards me. God has truly kept me!

I wrote this book to share with women across the world, the struggles I faced and overcame, and while writing, realized that each chapter represented God's purposeful design for my life. This thing called life has presented a few pleasing mountains and countless painful valleys. However, I have come to appreciate the meaning and beauty of each flower picked while in the valley — for it was there my purpose was revealed.

It became clear, the way I felt about myself, the quality of my relationships, my childhood environment, my attitude, my morals, and ethics, plus my ability to manage feelings and deal with difficulties all played a part in how much I meant [or did not mean] to myself. I soon learned that I existed in life trying to deal with and escape from what appeared to be my grim and problematic truth.

This book means a lot to me because it was written out of obedience to God and also because every page of this book represents fragments of my life's journey. I would like it to be used as an instrument to help women realize the importance and purpose of their design.

I have won the battle of irrelevance [hands lifted], which was not my battle in the first place; it was the Lord's (2 Chronicles 20:15)! I rest in this: God intentionally designed me in HIS image for a unique purpose!

I seek to enrich the lives of women by equipping them with the ability to move beyond their place of "stuck" and pray this book evokes change and reaches the heart of women everywhere. You must take your time to fully digest the contents, for in doing so, God will begin a new work in you as He has in me. I hope you enjoy reading, as I certainly enjoyed the time I spent with God writing.

Be blessed!

Introduction

I realized years ago — yes, literally a couple of years ago — I could not fully come into who I was until I healed. More importantly, I could not truly heal what I continued to hide. In other words, the only way I could break free from pain was to acknowledge, identify, accept, deal with, and finally let go of the wounds that had me bound. Listen, in order for me to earnestly let go, I had to unmask a myriad of feelings.

Let me speak from a personal place. The process of healing is painful, and what I have learned was that in order to recover from pain, I had to experience pain. In all honesty, I can admit that the pain of recovery was greater than the actual pain itself. What do I mean? Well, the work involved in my recovery required that I go places where I was not ready to travel and required that I dig in areas I was unwilling to unearth, but in order to heal, I had to dig, and I had to dig deep.

Let us take, for example, a toothache. A toothache is an unbearable discomfort that causes excruciating pain in and around the tooth. Without proper examination, you cannot be certain of what is causing the tooth to hurt; all you know is that it hurts! However, after the examination (digging), the endodontist identifies what appears to be an exposed nerve (the reason for hurt) that was caused by a badly decayed and infected tooth (pain). To address the exposed nerve, the endodontist will have to perform a root canal. During the procedure, the nerve is removed from the tooth, and soon thereafter, the pain is gone. The tooth is saved, but the nerve which caused the pain no longer exists.

When we think of a root canal, we automatically cringe. For me, however, the cringe was not brought on by the procedure but by the pain associated with the process. See, we often want to rid ourselves of the pain without going through the process. However, doing so will prevent proper healing and growth. I can undoubtedly speak to both the pain of a root canal and the pains associated with life, and just as an endodontist, I had to dig deep to get to the root of what was causing the hurt so that I could rid myself of the pain.

Moving Day

It was around 8:30 in the morning, and I was headed to Raleigh Durham International (RDU) airport. While exiting Interstate 540 West for the last time, I got a glimpse in the rearview mirror before changing lanes and could not help but notice the tightly packed belongings in the backseat of my car as well as the widely scattered thoughts roaming through my mind.

I began to question how I got to this place in life: What did I do wrong? Could this moment have been prevented? Would I ever see my friends again? Will I be okay? Will the pain ever go away? Why does it hurt so badly? While the questions were not difficult to answer, the responses to them were painful to accept.

My sister had purchased a one-way ticket from Louisiana to North Carolina and while it was always good to see her, this time, seeing her would be bittersweet. I parked at the airport terminal and began to grapple over what this moment would bring and realized that I was about to experience a drastic change that would adjust the entire course of my life forever!

While waiting, my phone rang. It was Freda calling to inform me that she was pulling up behind me. She wanted to see me off but was limited in time as she was preparing for deployment. We spotted my sister and motioned her in our direction. We all said our tearful goodbyes, and the two of us (my sister and I) headed to Cracker Barrel to grab a bite to eat before getting on the road.

9: 45 A.M.

We entered the restaurant, and to my surprise, two of my dear friends (Lisa and Lorraine) were seated at the entrance. I did not know whether to laugh, cry, to be happy, or sad. We greeted one another, I placed my name on the waiting list, and we began engaging in small talk, while waiting to be seated. Moments later my name was called. We stood up, and at the direction of the hostess was led to our seats. While on our way there, I could not help but notice how one tear after another began to fall from my eyes on what seemed to be one of the longest and most laborious walks of my life.

The reality of this moment was unreal. This would be my last breakfast as a North Carolinian. I was sitting there, choked up, trying to maintain my composure while pushing through all sorts of emotions, determined to wear a smile, hoping my fake smile and real feelings would somehow cooperate to make the moment more manageable. Instead, that fake smile, from time to time, was exchanged for a face full of tears. I was not ready for this. All that I had grown to know and love would soon become a distant memory. My mind and heart were at odds. Everything in me was fighting against this. My mind had not embraced the reality of what was taking place while my heart knew best and somehow accepted and developed an internal lens that revealed a bright future.

11: 15 A.M.

I did not want to ruin the last couple of hours I had in North Carolina talking about my moving away. I just wanted to tip out in silence because too much talk would cause an eruption of emotions that I was neither willing nor prepared to face. Instead, we sat around the table, reminiscing about the good times our friendship had endured. We were even able to discuss the purpose we each served in the lives of one another. At that moment, I gained an appreciation and understanding of the history that our conversations served — riveting talks that ultimately kept me spiritually grounded and mentally engaged.

Looking back on years of mutual spoken exchanges helped us to recognize the significant similarities of our lives — similarities that justified the spiritual connection of our appointed friendship. A friendship that compelled Lisa to organize this breakfast, despite finding out hours before my North Carolina departure. This was a gathering of meaning that confirmed how the 945 miles between us would unquestionably change our proximity, but never our position as friends.

12: 00 P.M.

We finished our breakfast, paid for our meals, and headed towards the exit. The time had finally come for my sister and I to get on the road to Louisiana. Wait a minute. . . this scary yet realistic moment could not be true as I had an extreme urge to jump on the interstate and head back to my apartment. However, the surety of the moment became apparent when I spotted my belongings piled up in the back seat of my car. This was it!

I began to feel a heaviness in my heart and a tightening in my throat as I mustered up the strength and courage to say goodbye. While driving off, tears fiercely fell from my eyes, and just like that, North Carolina became a memory as it slowly faded into the horizon.

DECEMBER 17, 2005: 3:30 P.M.

Big Sis and I drove nonstop for six hours and decided to sleep over in Atlanta so that we could be refreshed for the last stretch of our drive to Louisiana. We grabbed breakfast the next morning and then hit the road. Seven and a half hours later, we pulled up to a beautiful and thriving community full of lakefront estates, a community that I would soon call home.

For as welcoming and comforting as the community appeared, I could not help but think of where my strength would come as my entire life had shifted, and I had no idea how to obtain its [life's] balance.

Thoughtful Considerations

Have you ever had to make a life changing decision, if so, what was that decision?

_____

_____

_____

_____

_____

_____

_____

_____

_____

_____

_____

_____

_____

_____

_____

_____

_____

_____

_____

_____

_____

_____

Why did you make the decision?

_____

_____

_____

_____

_____

_____

_____

_____

_____

_____

_____

_____

_____

_____

_____

_____

_____

_____

_____

_____

_____

_____

_____

_____

What impact did it have on your life?

_____

_____

_____

_____

_____

_____

_____

_____

_____

_____

_____

_____

_____

_____

_____

_____

_____

_____

_____

_____

_____

_____

_____

_____

Fighting for Life

I was fortunate as a child to have lived in a community with a great deal of green space (park) situated in the middle of the neighborhood. This central spot was used as a gathering place for the laughter brought on by the innocence of child play and the artful chatter of grown folks' cheerful conversation. My beloved neighborhood was an assembly point in the community that forged involuntary friendships and produced bonds that resulted in a healthy and safe environment.

I wore nice shoes and clothes, had a meal for breakfast, lunch, and dinner with snacks in between, and always had a warm bath after outdoor play as a refreshing way to wash the day away. I was brought up in the church and remember those Easter and Christmas skits, those big hugs from the congregants, and the leaders who always wanted to know how school was coming along and would ask for one quoted Scripture from the Bible before heading on their way.

As a child, life was packed with educational programs that taught me how judicial bills were made, how to count, how to spell, grammar, vocabulary, and comprehension. Yet I was untaught on how life for me came to be. There were moments throughout my day where a parade of thoughts would flood my mind. I wondered why I called my aunt "mom" and how it is that I knew she was my aunt.

I questioned my father's presence (or lack thereof), knowing that my aunts' husband was not him. It was apparent that my biological mom and dad were not around; however, I was not aware of the reason behind their absence. So, there I was, an eight-year-old child, attempting to fit the pieces of my puzzling life together.

HERE TODAY AND GONE TOMORROW

She left me when I was only one month old. Her unexpected death deprived me of the opportunity to experience that unique and unmistakable bond that is shared between a mother and her child. I was too young to understand the circumstances surrounding her death, but as I grew older, I naturally became curious about the woman I never had the chance to know — the one who introduced me to life. I came to discover that she was beautiful, as evidenced by the cracked and faded black and white photo I held of her in my hand.

Unfortunately, I never had the opportunity of getting to know the intricate details of who she was or what she represented. Therefore, I did not know what part of me exemplified any part of her. I would never understand how she managed to maintain her beauty, how she kept every strand of hair in place, how she determined which lipstick to wear with what outfit, how she carried herself as a woman, or even her secrets of womanhood. I had an idea of how she cared for herself externally, but because I did not fully know who she was, I lacked an appreciation for what she carried internally.

Note to reader: It is crucial to understand how a mother fulfills an irreplaceable role in a child's life. A special bond is shared during pregnancy and beyond, as she (the mother) is an important symbol of connection for her baby. Studies show that babies quickly bond with their mothers and, at just hours old, recognize and respond to their mother's voice. Sadly, my mother's voice was as distant to me as her presence.

HERE ONE MINUTE AND GONE THE NEXT

He gave me away when I was only two years old. The abandonment of my father left me weak, vulnerable, and unassured. Did he not understand that I needed him? I often wondered what I had done to make him give me up so easily or what it was I could have done to make him fight hard to keep me. So, where was he — my father, that is? Did he know that he was responsible for shaping who and what I would become? Did he not perceive how the weight of his influence would form my image? Did he not care that one day I would need to look back on his demonstration of what a good relationship between a man and woman resembled?

The sad thing about it is that I never saw my father stare deep into the eyes of my mother. I never saw him open a door for her before they entered a building. I never saw him pull out her chair before they were seated. I never saw him walk to the right of her as a sign of protection. I never heard the phone ring with him calling to tell her he was on his way home from work. I never saw him embrace her with warmth upon his arrival. I never saw them sitting around the dining room table laughing as they talked the day away, and I never heard them having conversations of understanding and meaning.

None of this was visible, and it was not because I lacked the desire or that I was deprived of these memories, but instead, it was because I was stripped of the option.

DISJOINTED BY THE ABSENCE OF TIME

My mother was gone, my father was nowhere in sight, and without even knowing, my siblings were too. We were separated when my oldest brother was 14, my sister was 12, the youngest brother was 10, and I was two. *What should have been some of the brightest moments in our childhood turned out to be some of the darkest obstacles in our lives.* We were robbed of time and, therefore, unable to create lasting memories.

Reminiscing on things such as giggling in our rooms well past bedtime, tussling over the remote, playing indoor tag, helping one another with homework, hiding in those conspicuous spots in the house, or having those heart to heart sibling talks were activities that were nonexistent . . . well, for me anyway.

We shared no special occasions, such as birthdays and family parties, or cherishing moments of daily enjoyment like trips to the playground or snug bedtime stories. I do not even have memories of family dinners. None of this was possible because my siblings and I lived in different cities, but we might as well have lived on different continents. The gap between us was huge, and time kept making it larger. We were scattered all over the state of Texas, with hundreds of miles between us.

Not knowing my biological family eventually disrupted my foundation, and I began to struggle with security, safety, attachment, and low self-esteem. I was hypersensitive, had a fragile sense of self, and experienced intense feelings of loneliness and worthlessness. I would often mull over my existence, wondering why my siblings were so much older than me — maybe it was because I was not supposed to be. Was I a mistake? Was I the reason for my mother's death? Would she still be alive had I not been born?

My ten-year-old mind could not accurately answer the questions, so in an attempt to stop the thoughts from flowing, I took ownership, essentially blaming myself for my mother's death, my father's abandonment, and for being separated from my siblings. The thoughts were both painful and paralyzing and as time grew, so did my relationship with rejection. I felt invalidated and thrown away — mainly because I was unsure of who I was, and rightfully so, because I certainly was not sure of who they were (my biological family).

The sexual abuse, along with everything else I was trying to survive, subjected me to the unwelcome and unwarranted fondling of my private area. You know, that area that a mother and father firmly warned you to set boundaries around, boundaries that restricted entrance and, therefore, was off-limits. I did not know how to feel about the fondling, but I did know what I was feeling was not right. I knew it was wrong to be preyed upon by the very one positioned to protect, and as such, the image of family that I created in my mind was destroyed. Surely, this cannot be what family resembles! Why is this happening? How can I get it to stop? When will it stop? Whom can I tell? Will they believe me? What am I supposed to do?

I felt filthy and became a bit withdrawn. I needed to tell someone, yet never built up the courage, mainly because I did not know what effect the disclosure would have on the people involved. Besides, at that age, I did not know how to adequately explain the confusion surrounding the improper invasion of my innocence.

My sister and I had forged a relationship and by the time I was twelve, we had made countless visits to one another that took place during the holidays, spring and summer breaks (remember, we were hundreds of miles apart). As time passed, we started having conversations surrounding the possibility of me living with her once she graduated from college. Now, I heard what my sister said during our talks, but it was difficult to take what she said to heart. Not because I did not think she was sincere in what she said, but because I could not imagine living with someone I did not know, completely. I mean, I knew she was my sister, but who and what I was most familiar with were the people and life that I had grown to know and truthfully was not willing to move away from my questionable yet firmly rooted foundation.

I remember always being in church, which consisted of all-day fellowship on Sundays, Bible study, choir rehearsal, revival, convocation, and oh yeah (throwing my head back in laughter), the annual United National Auxiliaries Convention (UNAC) in Waco, TX. I would sit in church during UNAC anxiously awaiting melodies from the musical greats such as Commissioned, The Moss Brothers, The Clark Sisters, and The Winans. I was always in awe of how well-dressed the congregants were. They would have on their big hats, one-of-a-kind handbags with matching shoes, exquisite brooches, and nice tailor-made suits.

UNAC is where I met my first boyfriend. Well, so I thought. What did I know about relationships at such a young age? Especially since up until now, I had no proper demonstration of what one symbolized. We dated, or shall I say, talked on the phone for about a year, and without much notice, my life took a drastic turn; a turn made without my consent, and before I knew it, I was fourteen and living in North Carolina with my sister and brother-in-law. I questioned if I had done something wrong because the move from Texas to North Carolina was swift. Whatever the case, I was convinced of one thing: this was sure to add another layer to the already repressed layers of rejection that mounted in the recesses of my mind.

Out of routine, I found myself getting up on Sunday mornings, preparing to sit at the family table for breakfast before getting fully dressed for church, and would suddenly remember that I was no longer in Texas. Living in North Carolina was still very new and uncomfortable to me so, to find a level of comfort, I would stay locked up in my room until dinnertime, and while in there, would sit on my bed, wondering how my aunt was doing. Missing her laugh, those homemade sweets, and that sun-made iced tea. After dinner, I would clean the kitchen and head back to my room, this time, with tears in my eyes. I was homesick and longing for what once was.

I remember the awkwardness of each day, trying to fit in and adapt to a new family and a new environment. Conversations were difficult to hold because outlooks on life were different. North Carolina was hard and uncomfortable for me. It was like living in a different world, especially since our two worlds had suddenly become one. I was torn between them [worlds] and could not for the life of me figure out what caused their world to be so different from mine. Despite that, I seemed to have landed amid something great. However, I did not know how to navigate this new terrain, and I am sure it was difficult for them to navigate as well!

My sister and brother-in-law lived a nice life. They both had good jobs, stayed in a nice neighborhood, shared moments of their day, laughed together, vacationed every year together, were sensitive to the needs of one another, frequently went out on dates together, and just seemed to genuinely love one another. This was the life, which had now become my life too. I was right in the nucleus of what a true relationship echoed.

I can remember watching my sister getting dressed in the morning and was intrigued at how she applied her makeup, how well she dressed, and how confidently she walked as she graced the hallway wearing one of her designer perfumes. She was on her way to the kitchen to warm up the breakfast that my brother-in-law had prepared. He would hand my three-month-old nephew (Steven) to my sister, kiss her on the cheek and head out the front door carrying a cup of coffee in one hand and holding a briefcase full of *ungraded* test papers (laughing — love you brother-in-law) in the other.

I would soon head down to join them for breakfast, and my first stop would be my baby nephew. I would pick him up, kiss on him, and make him giggle a little before putting him back in his seat. We ate breakfast in almost complete silence and, once finished, would gather our belongings and head out the front door.

I would rush home from school every day just so that I could play with my baby nephew. I had taught him how to make the funniest faces, and when he would make them, we would both bust out laughing. Before long, we would wind down by watching television. A few hours later, he would lay his head on my chest and wrap his little baby arm around my neck (as if he knew a hug is what I needed at that moment) before falling off to sleep.

Three years later, my sister gave birth to my second nephew, Austin. We (my brother-in-law, Steven, and myself) visited my sister and Austin in the hospital. When I spotted Austin, I picked him up and lay his head on my shoulder (as if to ease my pain). With my hand supporting his back, I introduced myself to this new bundle of joy. My heart lit up when he wrapped his little hand around my finger. I must have held him in my arms for what seemed like hours. They (Steven and Austin) made my transition to North Carolina easier. They were my peace. I loved them, and guess what? They loved me right back, just as I was, broken and all.

I made average grades in school, dated guys my sister and brother-in-law detested, and associated with people with whom they did not approve. A couple of years after graduating from high school, my brother-in-law, sister, and I decided that it would be a good idea for me to spend some time getting to know my oldest brother, so I moved to Maryland. While there, I maintained two jobs, one of them at Value City, where I worked part-time and met Linda. Linda worked at the jewelry counter, and I worked in the women's department. We would take lunch together and often found ourselves talking about God. While I knew Him, I was not living a life that was pleasing to Him. No, I was not wilding out or anything, but will say that I was not living upright and had no problem with cussing a person up one side and down the other (thank God for deliverance)!

I remember Linda asking me during our lunch break one day how I thought it would make my aunt feel to know that I had such a foul mouth. I do not think she knows, but her question was responsible for the re-alignment of my walk with Christ. It was not long after that my five-year stay in Maryland ended, and I moved back to North Carolina, where I met the perfect gentleman, or so I thought.

Soon after moving back to North Carolina, I landed a job managing a fast food restaurant. It was about forty-five minutes to closing one weekend night with a few customers lined up at the drive-thru window. I checked on my crew, pulled the cash drawers to the dining area, and proceeded to the office to count down. There was a knock on the office door, and when I opened it, one of my crew members handed me a piece of paper with a name, number, and note requesting that I call. I tossed the paper aside and continued to count.

The last customer in the drive-thru had passed. I turned off the sign as formal notification that the restaurant was closed and we were cleaning in preparation to exit. Once the restaurant was cleaned, I went back to the office to set the alarm, grabbed the piece of paper off the counter, stuffed it in my pocket, turned off the lights, and we exited through the side door.

It was a few days later, and I figured I would call. His conversation was not the best, but he lured me in with his charm. He was a well-dressed, good-looking man with an incredible physique. We started spending time together and eventually became a couple. Things seemed to be going great, so much so that he moved in a couple of months later (red flag #1).

About a year and a half later, I decided that I wanted to change professions because the restaurant business was no longer fulfilling. I began looking for a new job, and while I was not sure of what I wanted to do, I did know that I wanted to be in an office setting. I filled out a couple of applications, and days later got a phone call for an interview in a city three hours away. I scheduled the interview, and a week later, we drove there. I was excited about the possibility of starting a new job and looked forward to the interview. We arrived in Raleigh that evening. I stopped at an Automated Teller Machine (ATM) to grab some cash so that we could get a bite to eat (red flag #2).

After dinner, we headed to the hotel, and upon arrival, I put my belongings down and hopped in the shower. When coming out of the bathroom, I noticed that neither he nor my car keys were in the room. When he returned, he explained that he had taken my car (red flag #3) to run to the store. I was deeply disturbed and baffled at how he figured he had the right to take my vehicle without my permission but was at a loss for words, so I just let it go.

The interview on the following day went well, and we headed home shortly after. A couple of days later, while paying bills, I noticed money missing from my account. I called my bank, and they were able to trace two evening ATM transactions made within two hours of each other during our two-day stay in Raleigh. He had stolen money from my account using my ATM card (red flag # 4). But when did he take the money, and how did he get my PIN? I played back the events of that day and remembered that I had not used much caution when stopping at the ATM (naïve because I did not grow up in an environment where it was necessary to look over my shoulder). I also remembered him not being in the hotel room when I came out of the bathroom from showering. Putting the two instances together confirmed that this is when and how he stole my money.

An array of emotions ran through my head. I was furious, confused, hurt, disappointed, and I felt betrayed. One day, the phone rang, and I answered to a kind voice on the other end, telling me that they would like to extend a job offer. I was excited (about the job offer) and troubled at the same time. Here I was about to embark on a new chapter of life while the person whom I thought I would spend it with had stolen money from me. I confronted him about the missing money, to which he categorically denied, further assuring me with his charm that he would never do anything to hurt me (remember that statement). For some reason, I believed him even though I had concrete evidence that proved otherwise!

A couple of years passed, and we were now living in Raleigh. The relationship had declined. However, my heart was in it by this time, and I can truthfully say that I loved the man. Until this point, I had never experienced such, and somehow managed to remember the teachings on love from early childhood — teachings that suggested how loving a person despite their wrongdoing was the antidote to changing that person's ways. I understood the teaching at that moment to mean that I was to continue loving him; you know, continue to show love until he became aware of the wrong, he was doing and, as a result, turn from it.

Not so! I frequently received insufficient fund notices from my bank, particularly a few days after payday. The phone calls from other women were constant, and the mental as well as physical abuse became a part of everyday living. I remember sleeping with my purse clutched to my chest as a way to secure my funds because he would take blank checks from my wallet and cash them out for hundreds of dollars at a time. In addition to that, I begin to see lip gloss, hairbrushes, and body lotions in my car that did not belong to me.

The evidence was blaring; however, I quickly learned to limit my conversation with him concerning his dishonest ways, as any conversation about it would result in violence.

Note to reader: The irony in this is that we hope to spark change in a person who is no good to or for us by loving them, despite how little they love us. Changing a person is not like investing in dilapidated property, mainly because investing in rundown property offers options — you can do with it as you please! As a matter of fact, you can give the property a new look from time to time, with as little or as much effort as you desire. I thought simply loving him would cause him to change his ways. Instead, years later, I realized that there is nothing anyone can do to change the mind or actions of a person. That change has to come from the willingness and desire of that individual. In other words, until a person wants to change, they will not!

The level of his deception and audacity was astounding. He would take my car while I was asleep and stay gone for days. I vividly recall a time that he was supposed to pick me up from my part-time job. It was around 10:30 at night, and as I exited the building, I grew concerned because he was nowhere in sight. I waited as one car drove away, then another and another. I was now the only person left, and as I stood there in the dark, I decided to give him a call. He did not answer, and I was not surprised. I did the only thing I knew to do, and that was to start walking home.

It [home] was not a far drive, but it was a long walk. As I got a little bit down the road, he pulled up behind me, asking me why I did not call. I could not give him an answer right then because I was juggling between anger, embarrassment, and fear.

When I got a sense of calm, I told him that I did call, but figured he did not answer because he was likely with another woman. What did I say that for? Because the next thing I remember was the taste of blood in my mouth from a busted lip. He had hit me. . . again.

After his apology, we decided to take a break from one another, and while it was a short break, I still availed myself to him mainly out of fear and guilt. A few days later, I picked him up from work and dropped him off where I presume, he lived. I went in to use the bathroom (but really to be nosey) and noticed another woman's belongings. I questioned him about the belongings, and of course, a fight ensued. Before I knew it, I was being hogtied. All I remember at that point was a blue bath sheet being wrapped around my face, obstructing my nose and mouth, making it hard for me to catch my breath. I was trying (with what little air I could gather) to tell him that I could not breathe, but he was not letting up. Resigning to defeat, I closed my eyes and resolved in my mind that I was about to die.

The moment I gave up, he gave in and untied me. I gathered myself but sensed his presence behind me, so I headed towards the front door at a fast and intentional pace. As I opened the door to exit the house, he pushed me over a low-lying balcony, which caused a scar (remains today) on my lower back. I figured he either pushed me to harm me or to stop me, probably both.

Year eight, and I am still with him, but nothing has changed. Actually, things had gotten worse. At this point, I was starting to believe all of the negative and humiliating things he had been saying to and about me. For years, he told me that I was nothing and how no one outside of him would want me. I remember giving him play-by-play accounts of his deceitful ways, and he would gaslight me by trying to manipulate me into questioning my sanity as a deflection. He would often tell me that there was something wrong with me and that I needed to see a psychiatrist. He continued his antics by accusing me of being a paranoid bipolar schizophrenic who suffered from hallucinations. I knew there was nothing wrong with me (or was it) and that he was just trying to tear me down with his controlling tactics. Even so, it was starting to work.

One Saturday afternoon, just as I was about to take a nap, the front door opened. It was him. He had come home to shower and change clothes before heading back out. He told me that he had been called into work. Everything in me knew he was lying, primarily because when he came out of the bathroom, he was clean-shaven, wearing a pristine, white shirt, freshly pressed khakis, and he smelled of cologne. I got an overwhelming desire to let him know that I knew he was lying, and while one part of me wanted to keep my mouth shut, the other part was pulling on me to say something. I was admittedly afraid to say anything and had made up in my mind to keep quiet.

As I walked out of the bedroom past him, I involuntarily blurted out to him that I knew he was not going to work but instead going to be with another woman. The next thing I know, I was being dragged fifteen feet away. I was face down on the carpet with the sharp of his knee in my lower back and his large hands covering both sides of my face. I was convinced that he was about to snap my neck and could feel the warmth on my cheek from the puddle of tears that formed in the carpet beneath my face. I was afraid to say a word thinking that word would be my last. All he had to do was slightly twist his wrist, and it would be over for me. I lay there, trying to understand why his abuse came at me as if it were something that he felt I deserved. All I could do was pray and cry, then suddenly, he released me from his grip and darted out the front door.

I got up and sat on the edge of my bed, holding myself while rocking back and forth vigorously. His words ruminated in my head. I felt like I was about to lose my mind, literally! Do not judge me, but I could hear and feel gears unwinding in my head. I saw the floating alphabet circling in my purview but could not put one letter with another to form a word. I felt that at any moment, I would implode. However, somebody somewhere had to be praying for me because I suddenly heard the subliminal voice of my aunt saying, "When you cannot do anything else, baby, simply call on the name of Jesus." I could not open my mouth to speak, yet willed my mind to hear my voice as I thought on the name of Jesus, repeatedly.

I had somehow managed to pull myself together and noticed I was standing in the middle of the kitchen, drinking a glass of water. I am not sure how much time had elapsed, but it seemed like forever. I plopped down on the living room couch and sat there for a moment staring into the air, trying to process ALL of what had just happened. This was nothing new and had been going on for the past six and a half years. However, for some reason, it was different this time. I could not make much sense of it other than I had allowed years of mental and physical abuse to infiltrate the very essence of my being.

I could not take this any longer. I needed to do something, I needed help. *No, I needed out!* I called Nita and briefly explained to her what had just happened. She insisted that I come to her place. I do not know why, but for some reason, I loaded every article of clothing and every pair of shoes I owned in the backseat of my car and headed to her house. On the ride over, I thought about how I had left two rooms of furniture in my apartment but quickly tossed that thought aside because I needed to strategize my next step. I figured I could simply move to a different apartment.

Nope, that would not work because, previously, during one of our breakups, I had decided to move to a new place only to come home and find him standing on the balcony of my second-floor apartment. How did he get there? He had no access to enter! Oh well, I was exhausted and could not process another thought. I just wanted to get some rest.

I pulled up to Nita's house, took out a few things, and headed inside. We talked until we fell asleep, and to be completely honest, I think I must have fallen asleep early into the conversation because I did not remember much of anything from that night. The next morning, we ate breakfast and talked some more. This time I was cognizant enough to remember that I shared with Nita everything that I had gone through with him up until that point. I also remember asking her not to share what we discussed with anyone, and she promised.

It was Monday morning, and as I was heading in to work, I received a call from my sister. I thought nothing of it because my sister and I talked regularly and even more so since she had left North Carolina years prior to move to Louisiana. However, on this particular morning, our conversation was different. She asked me if I would be interested in moving to Louisiana. Of course, I was interested (my escape from the horror that had surrounded me for eight years) but wait, not really! After all, I had finally landed my dream job and had a great circle of friends. So surely, there was some way I could stay in North Carolina without having to deal with his daunting abuse.

I mean, everything else in my life was great, so yeah, "I can make this work in North Carolina" were the thoughts that were playing in my head as my sister spoke. She explained that there was no need to give her an answer right then but that she would call back in a couple of days for my response.

As promised, my sister called me a couple of days later. I was still uncertain of what I wanted to do because, truthfully, I wanted to stay in North Carolina, but I knew leaving was necessary. I had mixed feelings. I wanted out of the relationship, just not in this way. I asked my sister for more time, and she agreed. In that extra time, I somehow convinced myself that I could escape the grips of mental and domestic abuse and that it was possible for me to live in peace (a reality that only presented itself outside of home).

About a week later, I was in my office, and the phone rang. It was my sister asking what I had decided. I still had not made up my mind and could only imagine my sister's frustration; however, she never expressed it and, in fact, remained very calm. We ended the call, and as soon as the receiver hit the base of the phone, I heard the voice of the Lord telling me that I needed to move. In obedience, I immediately called my sister back and reluctantly explained to her that I was ready to move to Louisiana (my sister knew to call me because Nita, even though she promised not to, had called to inform my sister of the abuse).

I had now gone through three stages of life: One, as a child trying to push through all the debris of rejection, abandonment, betrayal, and disappointment. Two, as a young adult dealing with mental and physical abuse, sanity, deceit, hurt, anger, and rejection. And three, having to alter my entire life as an adult just to live (all of which caused immense pain). Yep, fighting for my life had definitely become a normal part of living.

Note to reader: Some may wonder why I did not leave the relationship. While I desperately wanted to move on, it was not that easy We would break up from time to time (which was a huge relief and what I viewed as my way of escape), but I feared leaving him. We had been fighting for years, and I could not be sure of what my leaving would trigger or how it would affect my physical well-being. However, one of the points that I would like for you to take from this chapter is that I had to leave in order to live.

I found the courage to reach out to and receive support from family and friends so that I could break free of the violence. I encourage you to do the same. *Please be safe and call the National Domestic Violence Hotline at 1-800-799-7233 (SAFE) should you need.*

Thoughtful Considerations

What emotions or feelings of your past still exist?

_____

_____

_____

_____

_____

_____

_____

_____

_____

_____

_____

_____

_____

_____

_____

_____

How do those emotions or feelings affect your everyday life?

_____

_____

_____

_____

_____

_____

_____

_____

_____

_____

_____

_____

_____

_____

_____

_____

_____

_____

_____

_____

_____

_____

_____

_____

_____

_____

How are you managing these emotions and feelings?

_____

_____

_____

_____

_____

_____

_____

_____

_____

_____

_____

_____

_____

_____

_____

_____

_____

_____

_____

_____

_____

_____

_____

_____

_____

_____

_____

_____

Lost Hope

Once the angle by which I was to flow in this chapter was made known, I knew it would be hard to write.It took weeks of toiling before I finally yielded to exposing the hidden fragility of my faith. About eighteen months ago, God started dealing with me concerning [all] my hidden places and how concealing them would inhibit proper healing. Thus, I conceded and decided to swallow my shame so that I could expose my struggle. What I am revealing is a truth that I protected for years and honestly am embarrassed to admit; however, I feel it only fair to share with you the basis by which my truth (as it pertains to my faith), was clouded.

From childhood until about six years ago, life had thrown some pretty hard blows. Life did not play out for me like I thought it should; therefore, I felt that God had not shown up for me as I knew He could, and I routinely wondered why He even would. This pretext deepened and became the truth of my reality because the way I viewed life was anything but clear. My life was scattered all over the place, and there seemed to loom a vagueness surrounding the sketchy details of it. I needed to fully understand what to expect both *from* and *of* life so that I could live it.

In a quest for solace, I began to suppress experiences associated with my emotions by shutting off thoughts that provoked unpleasant feelings and displeasing monologues. I simply did not want to feel, and I thought this logic would produce an anesthetizing effect on my life — that it would eliminate the friction of thoughts that flowed in and out of my mind daily while changing the way I talked to myself *about me*. Instead, over time, this reasoning produced a false outlook on reality that prevented me from fully connecting with my feelings. As a result, I was disconnected from it all, and was oftentimes mentally and emotionally fatigued. As such, it was hard for me to know, understand, or even tap into positive feelings of happiness.

I remember as a child spending countless days and nights hoping that one day I would see my biological father, that I would be reunited with my siblings, and that the molestation would stop. As time passed, I tried tirelessly to make sense of my existence and understand my origin. All the while growing older and falling into a situation where I found myself constantly hoping for the violence to end — hoping that somebody someday would rescue me. Instead, what I experienced were decades of emptiness and unfulfilled hope.

My heart welled up with pain, anger, disappointment, and fear. I regularly felt the urge to scream . . . explosively. However, the intensity of that scream was often subdued with an eruption of silence that flowed like a hollowness throughout my entire body. It was an emptiness that eventually developed into hopelessness and nestled comfortably in the cleft between the two hemispheres of my brain.

I began to hold hope hostage, locking it away, desiring to smother its very existence. Thinking this response would control my dealings with its effects, as I did not want to become susceptible to the possibility of added disappointment. Therefore, I formed a resistance to it [hope]. Yes, I know hope comes easy for many, but for me, hope had let me down one too many times. It would show up, but it would never stay, just like my father! I wanted nothing to do with it because hope meant nothing to me and could do nothing for me. I wanted it to leave me just as it found me — empty!

Over the past decade or so, there have been many believers who have openly renounced their faith. Noticing this, I wondered how they could. How could someone go from being a devout believer to simply not believing at all? Could it be a disappointment in God, despair, self-admiration, an unexplained tragedy, misguided bitterness, or even worldly persuasion? Whatever the reason, I assumed that faith was lost because there had been a shift in focus related to the principles which guide the beliefs of an individual.

I can relate with many when it comes to the disappointment, discouragement, and the despair of life, and feel it only fair at this point to share with you the cloudiness that guided my principles. I thought that faith was the end-all be-all, but have since learned that it is one thing to have faith in God, but another thing entirely to hope in Him.

What am I saying? I am saying that I believed in someone whom I did not trust with my expectations. I believed in God and His existence but not necessarily in the fact that He would do for me what He promised. OUCH, that hurts! This revelation pierced my soul and caused me to question the authenticity of my relationship, wondering how I could have faith in Him on the one hand but was incapable of investing hope in Him on the other? How could I feel His presence and hear His voice, yet lack confidence in Him?

This admission was pivotal and marked the spot where my lesson and revelation came into play. I know what I just said is a bit hard to comprehend, but here is what I want you to know. Despite how difficult it was for me to admit, I would have to honestly say that standing in that place of prolonged obscurity pushed me to accept the discomfort of my unbelief. It brought me to this point!

Now, for you sanctified saints sitting in the back of the church wondering how this woman of God, who believes in God, could feel completely hopeless while relying on the power of prayer, fasting, miracles, signs, and wonders. Sit tight, because I am about to help a few of you comprehend this anomaly while, at the same time, I continue to help myself, too. In order to understand where I am coming from, you would first have to know where the fundamental disconnection between faith and hope existed for me. So, let's talk, and we will start with faith.

What is faith, exactly? Faith has both a complicated and powerful meaning. It is not loyalty based upon conditions being met. It is not even a power or a force that you tap into;

instead, faith is an assurance of trust despite obstacles; it is a persuasion, credence, or conviction that is measured by hope.

Hebrews 11 tells us that faith is being sure of what we hope for and certain of what we do not see. So, what does this tell me? It tells me that faith is a perspective, a point of view or a mental state of being that allows one to see their current situation as temporary while resting in the assurance of knowing that view is only preparation for what is to come. It is like trusting entirely in your future right now, even if there is no evidence to support your belief.

Being sure of what you hoped for reinforces and strengthens your relationship with God. The very presence of hope gives a sense of safety and security and suggests an opportunity for the future. Jeremiah 29:11 tells us that God knows the plans that He has for us — plans to prosper us, and not to harm us, plans to give us hope and a future. Well, I did not see nor trust that I would have a hope-filled future. Hope for me was a series of massive letdowns as there were many times my hope was coupled with praying, crying, snotting, and travailing; yet, nothing happened. I again would pray, cry, snot, travail, but this time would add a little of God's Word and fasting to the mix. Still, heaven was silent.

I began to second-guess the trustworthiness of God. I allowed my disappointments to become intertwined with doubt and was losing hope. I felt there was no effectiveness in prayer. So, I arrived at a place where I thought it was useless to pray (you all bear with me because this is just as painful for me to admit as it is for you to read). It was such an awful place to be, especially since prayer is an essential component of faith. Prayer is how my relationship with Him was nurtured. Yet, there I was without a prayer in my heart or on my lips.

Many years of unfulfilled hope and unanswered prayers landed me in this space. For a long time, I honestly felt that God was not on my side, that He was not hearing me and, frankly, that He cared not to. I had hoped to be rescued from the challenges of life only to find that answers to my earnest pleas were continually withheld. This disappointment, over time, deferred my hope and made my heart sick. I lacked peace, motivation, happiness, enthusiasm, determination, and aspiration — I found pleasure in nothing, and smiles were fleeting, phony, and sporadic, at best. They would only last for as long as I could bear to tolerate the effort it took to produce them. As soon as the smiles disappeared, my heart would again be filled with gloom.

What I hoped for had been put off so long that hoping in and for anything felt more like an affliction rather than a fulfilled expectation. Did God understand the toll that this unrelenting disappointment was taking on me? Did He even realize that my hope being postponed, prolonged, or put off, created a desire for me to hang on to something — anything that provided a sense of security? What I needed was bigger than a desire. I needed something immovable and sure!

So, faith comes from hearing and hearing by the word of God. But wait! Faith had to be based on something more than what I had heard. I had been hearing all my life, yet nothing had changed! Could it be that I lacked faith because I perceived what I heard versus giving my attention to what was being said? The last sentence of Romans 12:3 mentions how God has given each believer a measure of faith, and while this verse speaks mainly about pride, it helped me see that I did not truly understand faith, and, because of that, I thought I lacked it. However, according to this Scripture, faith is something that already exists, which let me know that my issue went deeper than faith and instead rested in my inability to hope.

I know, I know . . . faith and hope are intertwined, but is it possible to have one without the other? Yes, you can have faith without hope, but there is no way you can have hope without faith. Hebrews 11:1 gave us a macro view of this but let me flush this thing out by giving you a micro view. Faith is trusting God by believing in what He has promised. Hope is the anticipation that keeps our faith alive while waiting on the promise. So how then are promises manifested? Would you believe that it is not hope that manifests the promise but believing that does? Therefore, to have faith in something, there must first be a promise, which ignites feelings of expectation and desire (hope).

If you, too, would be honest with yourself, you will admit that no matter how many Scriptures you quote, how prolific your teaching, or how much sanctification you profess to have, every now and then, even the best of us, the holiest of us, and the most committed and anointed of us, will experience a lack of faith or hope.

About two and a half years ago, God said these things to me; I need you to lean in and low crawl (get low). I studied up on it and took it to mean that I needed to draw close to Him because there was something He was trying to get to and pull out of me (exchange). This request required a great deal of reliance on Him because, to do it, I had to trust Him (know that I was covered). So, God was requiring me to go from a position of standing to a position that placed me flat on my belly! The fascinating thing about changing your posture is that it involves trust — a total dependency.

He wanted more of me. He wanted me to trust Him with my life. He wanted me to rely on Him, confide in Him, feel safe, and be secure in Him. He wanted me to know that it was in Him that my hope was found. I now know this to be the intimate part of faith that I was missing, which equates to a total surrender grounded in hope. Hope's strength rests in God's faithfulness. This is why the memory of what God has done in the past is so powerful. It is that memory that reinforces our grip. Surely, if He did it before, He will absolutely do it again!

This takes me back to when I was living in North Carolina, and Freda dragged me out to church. I was having a rough time and called myself taking a break from God. I still loved Him but was upset with Him. I did not want to be in anyone's church service . . . you hear me! Anyway, we arrived at church, and I sat in the back because I did not want to be seen by anyone, not even by God (I had to laugh at this myself; how could I hide from the omniscient God?). As the service was coming to a close, I heard a voice calling out from the pulpit. He pointed directly at me and said, "Would the young lady with braids in her hair stand up?" I just sat there.

A few seconds later, the same voice spoke again. "Would the young lady with braids in her hair who is wearing an olive suit stand up?" Still, I did not move. He began walking towards me and said for the third time, "Would the young lady with the braids in her hair with the olive suit, sitting next to the young lady with the white suit, stand up?"

I could no longer ignore the call, and as I stood up, he directed me to meet him in the center aisle. He told me (even back then) that all God wanted from me was a total 'YES' (which requires full trust), and once He received that from me, everything in my life would fall into place.

Guess what? I had trust issues and will openly admit that I only had enough faith to hold me for the space and place that I was in — I had nothing to hold on to and soon conditioned my mind of the same. So, here I am years later, still dealing with trust, but what I have learned and continue to learn is to take God at His word. Some days will be easier than others, especially since life is full of minor frustrations and major disappointments, but none of us will ever be able to say, I hope in God without fail. You know why? Because we fail, we fall, and we put our hope in man.

Learning to hope in God is not a one-and-done event but an ongoing life journey. Your journey to achieving faith and hope in God may not mimic mine. For me, going on a twenty-one-day fast, meditating on Scriptures that spoke on faith (Scriptures that defined and demonstrated miracles of faith), having weekly Bible studies about the character of God, prayer, and therapy have helped to open my eyes to His goodness and made it easier to trust in Him wholly!

Yes, I talk to God *and* a Christian therapist! I know some will disagree, and it is fine if you do, but what I have come to know is that faith and therapy can occur simultaneously. Receiving therapy does not mean that I am compromising my faith or that my belief in man is greater than my faith in God. A therapist could never replace who God is in my life. However, he or she can provide me with the necessary tools needed to eliminate and or cope with emotions designed to inhibit my growth.

Not everyone who experiences similar issues will need the same resources as I used to overcome. Some who pray may overcome their situations instantly, while others require a bit more help. I truly believe that God knew this and gifted people to function in this capacity for that reason.

I encourage you not to travel alone; surround yourself with people who genuinely love you, who uphold you in prayer, who encourage you, and who rejoice with you. I want to challenge you to get and stay in your word — it will sustain you! I am learning to focus not on how my life will serve me, but more specifically, how God wants to use my life to be of service in the kingdom. Consider this truth; hoping in God comes from knowing Him intimately.

Note to reader: When you have a prolonged period (in some cases, years) of unanswered prayers, you begin to become comfortable in and with despair. Therefore, unknowingly, you perpetuate your own unhappiness by strengthening the trauma you are so desperately trying to escape.

Thoughtful Considerations

Have you ever lost hope in what was promised? Be specific. What was the consequence of that? What did you learn from that experience?

_____
_____
_____
_____
_____
_____
_____
_____
_____
_____
_____
_____
_____
_____
_____
_____
_____
_____
_____
_____
_____
_____

Can you think of a time when your faith wavered? If so, what do you think caused it?

_____

_____

_____

_____

_____

_____

_____

_____

_____

_____

_____

_____

_____

_____

_____

_____

_____

_____

_____

_____

_____

_____

_____

_____

What do you feel you can do to get past a sick heart that is brought on by deferred hope?

_____

_____

_____

_____

_____

_____

_____

_____

_____

_____

_____

_____

_____

_____

_____

_____

_____

_____

_____

_____

_____

_____

_____

_____

Rooted in Rejection

I struggled to write this chapter. I picked the manuscript up and put it down several times throughout the past couple of months. I would get in a good groove of writing and then weeks later experience a discontinued desire to express and expose my issues. Writing this book has been like pitting one force against the strength of another, where the force of my mind would weaken the strength of my heart. You see, my heart was willing to reveal a few intimate accounts of my life, but my mind refused! My mind was trying to comprehend how others would receive my written words.

More specifically, how was I to inform, inspire, and influence others without any formal training? All the while, deep down inside, I knew that my personal experiences made me relatable, and therefore, gave me reach. What am I trying to say? Experience teaches! Consequently, I decided to let my experiences coupled with my heart — you know, my character and integrity — be the voice that speaks.

In chapter two, we discussed how and why rejection formed. Now, in this chapter, we will discuss how it became rooted in my life. Our experiences with rejection might differ completely. For me, it was growing up in a world absent of my origin; I lacked an attachment to them simply because I spent no time with them and, therefore, did not know them. I felt rejected and inadequate, not because of my upbringing, but because I did not know or understand who I was. Not knowing this caused me to create my own narrative of life — a story that planted in me a relentless pursuit of purpose as it relates to my existence.

It appeared to me that my birth created death. I viewed my mother's passing, my father's abandonment, the unexplained separation from my siblings, oh, and let us not forget the unwelcomed fondling from a family member as death because each circumstance caused parts of me to die — fallen parts that nurtured the perfect petri dish of rejection.

I would first like to explain rejection from my point of view before I discuss how it was rooted in me. I am wise enough now to know that maturity, not age, was responsible for me coming into the awareness of rejection and the part it played in and on my life. Rejection is a painful emotion that is inevitable to escape. The funny thing about rejection is that it is normal and is something you will be faced with at some point in life.

Rejection will come masked as people not supporting your vision, a father never coming around, a mother never showing love, a boss disregarding you for a promotion, friends overlooking you for a group outing, being ignored, being walked out on, being turned down, being told you are not wanted, or maybe even being told or made to feel that you are not good enough.

Rejection stings and suggests a lack of value that often makes us question things about ourselves, mainly our self-worth, and can lead to unwise decision-making, which can sometimes take a lifetime to recover from. However, it is how we process rejection that makes the difference. Wait, before you put the book down, hear me out. I am by no means trying to minimize rejection, nor am I seeking to diminish its effects. I am merely trying to emphasize that rejection will show up, but it does not have to be as debilitating to your life as it was to mine.

Now, you know that my existence was nurtured in rejection, and as a child, I was unable to express or effectively identify the feelings I felt. As a result, I allowed my analyzed thoughts to become my reality by associating the adverse events of my life, whether actual or imagined (I developed opinions of myself based upon what I perceived to be true), to my existence. What do I mean by that? Well, I took the blame for the adverse circumstances of my life, which was an unconscious behavior I used as a coping mechanism to replace the negative thoughts I had surrounding my existence.

My thoughts were so intense that they tended to invade and take over my mind. I needed to calm the chatter in my head, so I began to sort my thoughts into questions. Questions such as "Why me? Why did my mother die? Why did my father abandon me? Why was I separated from my siblings? Why was I not wanted? Why was it ok to be molested? What did I do wrong? What was wrong with me? Was I a mistake?" The sad thing is that I began to answer all those questions on my own and some, if not all of the answers, started me on my journey to rejection.

How did I begin this journey, you ask? Well, no one corrected my faulty way of thinking mainly because no one knew what I was thinking. I would, from time to time, ask what happened to my mother. I was asking because I wanted to rid myself of the guilt. I needed to pull down the thoughts in my head that were always suggesting her death was a direct result of my birth. When I finally received an answer, it was that she died from an overdose of anesthesia. I wanted more, but that was all I was given. I needed a descriptive, substantive, and detailed account, like why was she under the influence of anesthesia? I felt knowing the answer to this question would lift my burden.

A little time passed, and my curiosity grew; I then asked why my mother was under the influence of anesthesia and was told that she was having a tubal ligation. Oooooh boy, here we go! This was the proof I needed to solidify my thoughts. I began associating the tubal ligation with her not wanting any more children, but more specifically, her not wanting me. You see, there are four of us, and while the three of them were two years apart (wanted), I was fourteen years younger than my oldest sibling (unwanted).

My mother did not want any more mistakes, and therefore she was having her tubes tied. I began rehearsing the thoughts and feelings of not being wanted in my head, which eventually created a diminished sense of self. Before I go on, keep in mind these thoughts and feelings are based strictly on privately drawn conclusions. No one ever said those things to me, confirmed my thoughts, or even knew what I was thinking.

It is important to note that the face of a mother is the mirror of the daughter and the place where the initial self-image is captured. This is when the daughter is assured of her value; however, I had no assurance, as I do not recall those mirror image moments. Hopelessly, I started to wonder what life would have been like had I lived it with her. I do not know, maybe I was too young to understand the weight of the answer to this question, so I ended up carrying it with me well into my adulthood. However, by this time, self-blame and self-criticism developed and had grown into a natural part of who I had become.

I recall having a couple — well, let me be real, many — conversations with my sister around the age of seventeen regarding romantic relationships that had ended. And, get this, these were not conversations centered on a whole bunch of breakups; instead, they were several conversations that took place due to a single breakup. I would question the action, which is normal, but because of where I was in life, I would automatically figure that I was the reason for the breakup. I went through an exhaustive search, dissecting my every action, all day long, for days at a time, trying to identify my deficiencies so that I could come to some sort of conclusion as to why the relationship did not work out.

This way of thinking became so routine that it consumed me. Every circumstance that did not play out as I expected would result in my going into a downward spiral of overthinking. It was so bad that if I did something as simple as speak to a person and they did not respond with the same level of enthusiasm, I would automatically take the blame, figuring that my tone must have been a problem; had I spoken *this way* instead of *that way* maybe their enthusiasm in responding would have matched mine. I would over-analyze every discussion, all facial expressions, and the body's conscious and unconscious nonverbal movements.

Talking was fatiguing because my mind would be on a high-speed chase from the beginning of a conversation to the very end and beyond. One word would pummel me, and I would become so motionless that I could not think past it . . . the word that is. Because of how I had trained my thoughts, I felt the need to over-explain and justify my every move. Rejection was so seated in me that every step I took, it followed. Boundaries were difficult for me to establish. As a result, I spent a lot of my time and energy pleasing others, which caused even greater displeasure within myself. I felt that I had no control over my life and was instead, being controlled by the overpowering thoughts of my mind.

I can remember times when it would take everything in me to sit up in bed. Did you hear me? I did not say it took everything in me to get out of bed; I said it took everything in me to sit up in bed. Why is that, you ask? Well, my mental health was not the healthiest. I fought and clawed internally to calm my mind, but I discovered that rejection had settled there and conspired with my thoughts to form deceit — a deceit that shadowed how I perceived every circumstance in my life. As a defense mechanism, I would repress my emotions as a strategy to shut off my thoughts. I would reconcile the negative thoughts and feelings that I harbored in my head and my heart by justifying, minimizing, and explaining them away as if they never existed.

My repression strategy did not work; instead, it brought about intense feelings of being misunderstood, created a mound of unattended emotions (that strengthened over time), and ultimately affected the quality of my life.

I began masking those unattended feelings with impulsive shopping that was often a secret drug I used to dull the pain. While the daily shopping provided me with temporary external relief, it seemed impossible to escape the immutable destruction that was taking place internally. It dawned on me that I only seemed to be doing well because I had tactically disguised my appearance (as if that made me whole) to offset what and how I felt about myself. I did not realize how my deceptive thoughts would make their way to my soul and how those thoughts began shaping the actions of my heart.

My esteem was low, and that made it difficult for me to accept compliments. My discomfort with compliments did not rest in the fact that there was no truth in what was being said; instead, it rested in my not believing the truth of what had been said. Simply put, a compliment went against everything that I thought, felt, and believed about myself. I saw the negative in everything, and as such, became this person who could function externally but was nonfunctional internally.

I spent a lot of time pondering what I had done wrong down through the years to deserve such fate. I wanted, no . . . *I needed* to change my life's trajectory, so I decided to dig deeper and connect with myself on a more intimate level. Wait, let me explain. I knew the surface me but had no relationship with the inner me and discovered that for me to gain a relationship with myself, I needed to change the way I viewed me, you know, reframe my thoughts. Therefore, I began to examine my thought soundtrack, and in reviewing it, identified many negative thought patterns on replay that needed to be taken out of the rotation. I challenged those thoughts and began associating them with events of my life.

Let me warn you, this is a very painful but necessary step as it allowed me to put a name to my feelings and helped me to understand what sparked my thoughts. Doing this helped me to acknowledge my emotions and made it easy for me to pinpoint what triggered them in the first place.

In a moment of transparency, I permitted rejection to be the self-inflicting catalyst that ruined over half of my life. Actually, I was just delivered from rejection about three years ago and concluded that it only existed because I allowed it and all of its layers — hurt, abandonment, molestation, pain, disappointment, fear, resentment, and anger — to take up space in my mind and wreak havoc in my soul. My deliverance did not come until I pushed through all of the garbage to stand firmly on the fact that I am who defines me and not my emotions or circumstances. Only then was I able to heal from the effects of its oozing wounds. You cannot escape rejection; it will show up at some point. However, you must dig deep and find the strength to push past it.

Thoughtful Considerations

All of us have faced rejection of some sort in life. What rejection have you experienced?

_____

_____

_____

_____

_____

_____

How did that rejection show up in your life?

_____

_____

_____

_____

_____

_____

_____

_____

_____

_____

_____

_____

_____

_____

_____

_____

_____

_____

_____

_____

_____

_____

What steps are you taking to push through rejection? How did you overcome it?

_____

_____

_____

_____

_____

_____

_____

_____

_____

_____

_____

_____

_____

_____

_____

_____

_____

_____

_____

_____

_____

_____

Forgiven Me

This chapter addresses my experiences and processes as it pertains to forgiveness and is designed to speak to those who are not quite in that place. You know, the place where the negativity of your past no longer controls you. The place where you are no longer subjected to those recycled feelings, thoughts, emotions, and behaviors, no matter how near or far they are from your present.

Speaking to and with women over the years, I have discovered that we all have very similar pains, some of which were suffered in silence — a silence associated with the stigma of exposure, guilt, and or shame. Truth be told, my greatest struggle in writing this book was unveiling parts of me that I held close. One, because of the vulnerability associated with the exposure, and two, because of the unwarranted judgment that follows.

My passion is in reaching women, more specifically, the minds of women, and positioning them to move beyond their place of *stuck*. I focus on this because I was once that woman. I was stuck in a place controlled by my emotions, emotions that strangled the life and living out of me. I was passing through life aimlessly without any regard or purpose. You know, just going through the motions.

In the chapter, *Lost Hope*, I discussed healing and the need to expose pain. In this chapter, I will go a bit deeper because it was at this point in life that I realized I could not be free until I was released from the damaging emotions of my past. In other words, liberation would not come until I had reconciled my relationship with yesterday. A reconciliation that gave me the ability to reach the balance needed so that I could move on with and in life. Freedom required me to understand the experiences associated with my past so that I could make sense of my feelings and pinpoint the circumstances upon which my emotions depended.

Many, if not all, of you reading this book have been confronted with challenges in life. Some of you begin facing them as an infant, as a toddler, as a pre-teen, as a young adult, or some may even be facing challenges right now as an adult. Well, if you can recall, challenges for me began when I was an infant, and as I grew into early adulthood, my challenges grew too.

I can remember a time as an adult when I was driving home from work. It was evening rush hour, and I was traveling about forty-five miles per hour. In preparation for the upcoming standstill, I began to slow down, when out of nowhere, the driver of a black Hyundai cut me off and slammed on their brakes. I also hit my brakes, barely escaping a rear-end collision. The space between my front and the driver's rear bumper was little to none. I instantly grew angry. Thoughts began brewing in my mind, and I quickly hopped out of my car to release from my head what was on my heart. I began to tap on the window gesturing for the driver to roll it down while simultaneously increasing the pitch in my voice, which was made evident by the looks of concern from drivers who were positioned two lanes away. I was disturbed by the incident but not disturbed enough to acknowledge and disapprove of my own misconduct.

While still making my way home, I phoned Angie to give her an account of what had recently happened. She listened intently and responded in a way that I was not expecting to receive. I thought she would certainly understand my anger, but instead, she asked, "What is wrong with you?" She continued by letting me know that my behavior on this day was not much different from the behavior I had displayed on most days. She then asked, "Is everything okay with you?" And then said, "This is not like you. What is going on with you?"

The phone grew silent. I had no answer to give. We ended the call, and I began to take account of what had happened throughout the course of my day, or, as a clearer point of reference, what had been happening in my life up until this day. I realized my faith-based foundation that had always informed my actions had been breached. I was a bubbly, warm-hearted, friendly, generous, kind, energetic, thoughtful, respectable, and well-mannered person who knew and showed love, but somewhere along the line, something had altered.

Something did not feel right! I was unhappy and resentful and did not know why. It was puzzling to me because a person who had a great support system of family and friends, good health, a good job, a nice car, a nice place to live, food on the table, and clothes on my back, should have no reason to demonstrate signs of unhappiness, yet, I did.

Note to reader: It is important to know that material things do not make a person happy; they only serve to accentuate happiness.

I felt "off" and began to take inventory and asked God to help me with my feelings. I needed to understand why I was so unhappy and why my actions were the exact opposite of what I knew to be right. I went from being gentle-spirited and kind-hearted to becoming cold-hearted and calloused. I needed reassurance so I called Freda. Our conversation was weighty, and right in the middle of one of her sentences, I interrupted and asked her if she was happy, and if so, what did being happy feel like? "Yes," she responded and explained happiness to be like an unending stream of gratitude that flowed throughout the body — a flow that left the heart feeling light. My response to her was that I always felt the complete opposite, indifferent and heavy.

I continued by explaining to her that my emotions were all over the place — how my temper was short, that it took nothing to set me off, and that I was always locked and loaded, prepared for battle, and poised for the next attack!

After entering my home, I sat down on the couch with tears running down my face. My heart was heavy, and my mind was full but blank. I was so mentally drained that I became physically fatigued, producing a weight my body could no longer withstand. I was about to buckle under pressure and needed God to understand that I could no longer carry this load, so I sat quietly for what seemed to be forever, wondering what was causing me to feel and react in this way.

I finally made my way to the bedroom in hopes of getting some rest, but the thoughts that filled my mind would not allow it. I was so full of unsolicited thoughts that my head felt like a 1000-pound brick that lay uncomfortably on the pillow. I tossed and turned throughout the night, and at some point, succeeded at drifting off to sleep.

It had been a restless night, and I lay there preparing my mind to rise from bed, but my body resisted. I was struggling, trying to pull myself together. I continued to lay there, sinking in my beds center, body motionless, trying to get my mind and body to come into agreement. I began to question if God saw me and if so, did He realize what was going on with me? Did He hear me and, if so, was He listening? I was at my wit's end. I did not know what to think and needed to know what it was I was to do to find some level of calm.

Dragging myself out of bed one limb at a time, I sluggishly made my way into the bathroom, where I caught a quick glimpse of my puffy eyes, which were caused by the tears that had fallen from my face throughout the night. Tears that had become the voice behind my words. As I leaned in a bit closer, I saw a reflection of what I had become. I had become a person who hid behind smiles meant to obscure hurt, insecurity, brokenness, and defeat. Mentally, I was a mess! Sadly, I had grown into a raging, insecure female who sought constant validation, trusted unusually quickly, and loved far too deeply. I lived much of my life buried under the guise of hurt and pain, which produced those frequent, sporadic, and impulsive fits of rage.

I needed help! I needed this to be fixed! No, *I needed to be fixed!* As a result, I began to pursue support through the process of introspection. I needed to go into the hollows of my mind to research those thoughts, and in doing so, I gave myself permission to freely get in tune with what I was feeling. Delving deep would allow me to acquaint myself with, identify, and name the emotions attached to my pain.

Let me be clear. This is not a one-and-done activity that takes place in forty-five minutes. It is a process that takes work.

Note to reader: I would like you to understand that it is what comes after the process that really matters. It's not the survival of the process that makes you stronger, it is the work that you put in as a result of the process that does.

Identifying my emotions required that I sit in the depth of the pain that I sought so hard to ignore. It also required that I get in touch with my emotions which allowed me to expose and singularize the feelings that had entangled me.

At this juncture, I was stuck. What is worse is that I was left with a fresh, uncomfortable perspective on my newly identified feelings — ones that were magnified by subsequent emotions, which caused injury to old wounds. I could feel the sludge that was nestled in the deep, dark corners of my heart. The same sludge that I was supposed to be moving past was instead sitting right amid my emotional residue, causing me to revert to repression.

Not too many days from then, I was walking at a nearby park and noticed gardeners planting flowers in the botanical. I was reminded of a biology lesson learned in high school. Specifically, it was the lesson about the growth process of a plant contained within a seed. Let me give a brief overview. A seed is planted in soil and is nurtured by water. The first sign of a well-nurtured seed is a small root that sprouts from it. The small root then continues to grow downward until it is firmly anchored in the soil while the shoot grows upward in the opposite direction, breaking the soil's surface, producing a developed plant.

Now, let me put this analogy into practical terms by linking it to my work on introspection. My identified emotions of rejection, abandonment, molestation, disappointment, fear, resentment, and anger were the seeds that had been planted in my heart by the thoughts that formed in my mind. Over time, those same thoughts grew with intensity and became the water that nurtured those emotions, which eventually sprouted into bitterness. It then became apparent that my harvest was a direct reflection of what I had planted.

Things were beginning to make sense, but what next? I was aware of how bitterness developed, but how was I to get rid of it? Well, I had to expose what was planted in the soil so that I could be healed. The exposure would uncover that hidden sludge which was responsible for how I was feeling, and forgiveness would destroy them. Forgiving is difficult, and while I am fully aware of the buzz surrounding the topic (as it has been discussed ad nauseam), I wonder if we are getting it, well, at least from the perspective by which I am presenting it.

My goal is to deliver a clear understanding of forgiveness, so I would like to start with its definition. The dictionary defines forgiveness as "ceasing from anger or bitterness towards another for an offense committed." Now, let me slow down right here and dive a bit deeper into this forgiveness thing. Forgiveness, to me, is giving up the expectation that your past could somehow play out a different way. The act of forgiving someone may be challenging, but the act of not holding on to what has been forgiven is an even greater challenge.

Simply put, forgiveness is not an automatic healer of emotions because our feelings may or may not line up with our decision to forgive, especially since hurt is very delicate, and pain runs deep. It takes time and is a process that begins with an intentional decision to release that which has been forgiven. A process that also involves surrendering to the attachments associated with those released memories. However, in order for the act of forgiveness to be effective, it must come from a place of authenticity.

It is critical to understand that choosing to forgive does not mean that you are letting the offender off the hook. It does not mean that you are permitting or excusing the offense. It does not even mean that you are playing the offense down by pretending that it never happened.

Instead, forgiveness enables you to embrace the pain you suffered without letting it define you. Forgiveness requires you to participate in the process of releasing the damaging feelings, thoughts, emotions, and behaviors associated with the offense.

Now that we understand forgiving someone as a process of releasing, I would like to challenge you to switch gears and give some thought to self-forgiveness. Listen, I get it. One of the hardest things to do is to forgive the offender for an offense. But what about the will of mind it takes to forgive yourself for holding on to the feelings associated with that which caused the hurt in the first place? We usually find it difficult to forgive ourselves; however, self-forgiveness is necessary. Truthfully, I initially felt I had nothing to forgive myself for, but I did.

I needed to forgive myself for owning the actions of the offender. I needed to forgive myself for harboring unidentified emotions for as long as I did and for letting those unidentified emotions take root in my heart, cultivating in me something and someone I was not. I needed to forgive myself for the constant bouts of self-blame and self-criticism. However, the beauty of self-forgiveness is that I was able to surrender to my present moment by letting go of the guilt associated with my past.

So, let us recap how forgiveness gave me life. Forgiving the offense of the offender released me from the shame, while forgiving myself for owning and harboring the emotions associated with the pain enabled me to let go of the guilt. I am what hurt me the most and, therefore, was responsible for unlearning the emotions associated with my pain. I had to forgive not only my offender, but I had to forgive me, too. I am now coming back to show others the way to their freedom as well. This freedom has afforded me the opportunity to become my authentic self without the desire to adjust who I am simply to fit another person's standard. I finally understand happiness and can therefore take responsibility for it by no longer making it the obligation of others.

Coming into the realization that the pain of my past was a part of my history and was in no way associated with my destiny empowered me to walk in liberty to fulfill my God-given purpose! I pray liberty for you, too!

Thoughtful Considerations

Why do you think forgiveness is so hard?

_____

_____

_____

_____

_____

_____

_____

After reading this chapter, do you feel you have anything you need to forgive yourself *of* or *from*? If so, what?

_____

_____

_____

_____

_____

_____

_____

_____

_____

_____

_____

_____

_____

_____

_____

_____

_____

_____

_____

_____

_____

How do you think forgiving others, as well as yourself, will impact your life?

_____

_____

_____

_____

_____

_____

_____

_____

_____

_____

_____

_____

_____

_____

_____

_____

_____

_____

_____

_____

_____

_____

_____

_____

Loving Me

They say time heals ALL wounds, and while this cliché is often true, in my case, time aggravated a few of them. In fact, time had become a safe haven by which self-blame and self-criticism magnified in my soul.

I thought becoming aware of my negative thoughts and linking them to my life circumstances was all that I needed to manage and eventually eliminate my pattern of negativity. While I had made great stride, I still had work to do, and because of that, my shopping continued, so as the space in my closet grew smaller, the battle with my emotions grew larger.

The true essence of my existence is what I lacked. I identified myself based on the relationship I had with pain. It hurt all over, but I carried no visible sign of it — it was a hurt that the human hand could not extend far or wide enough to touch. No one could see that I was hurting, nor could anyone see where it hurt. All that was seen is what I allowed and what

I allowed appeared to be free of any wreckage. However, my internal self was tattered, fragmented, and in total ruin.

My thought process had developed into a personal belief system that intrinsically became my value system. A concept that translated into me being very critical of me. Realizing this, I spent a lot of time reflecting on my character, actions, and motives attempting to disconnect myself from an identity that had been disrupted with thoughts of blame and criticism. So, there I sat — doubtfully believing in me, trying to disassociate myself from the likeness of self-doubt, hoping to find a safe place of belonging. Carrying the heavy and demeaning feelings of insecurity weighed me down and made going through life exhausting. Often, I shrank into the background and hid in obscurities because I did not want to expose to others those areas I tried to hide from myself.

I hated looking in mirrors, but it is not for the reason you think. I had no problem with my outer appearance. The source of my difficulty stemmed from my inner appearance. There were times when I looked in the mirror and caught a reflection that pierced right through me. It was in those times that discord undeniably existed between my inner and outer self. The conflict I am referencing is not the typical power struggle between thoughts and the reaction to those thoughts. Instead, I am talking about the internal battle incited by fear, inhibition, and self-doubt; thoughts that brewed in my soul like explosives in development.

It had gotten to the point where I did not even want to live. There were nights that I would cry myself to sleep with thoughts of suicide preoccupying my mind. I remember times while driving, being tormented with the idea of running head-on at high speed into oncoming traffic. This was not something that I had planned to do, but thoughts would come out of nowhere and take over, activating an intense conversation in my head. The conversation would abruptly end by the sudden and swift disturbance of force that hissed in my left ear as I passed the very vehicle I thought would be the death of me.

I was depressed and had sunk to a deep dark low. I always felt sad, disinterested, lonely (even with people around), hopeless, and discouraged. My sleep pattern changed. I went from sleeping through the night to barely sleeping at all. It often felt as though I was trapped under the weight of life from which I could not escape, and it was probably because that thing that served as a base to my self-belief was weak. Give me a moment to break this down, as what comes to mind is the foundation of a home.

The foundation is what a house is built upon and serves as the cornerstone that holds up and holds together the structure above it. One mistake in the foundation will cause even the most splendid of structures to fall. A poorly constructed foundation cannot accommodate the weight of a well-built frame as the foundation's poor construction will eventually transfer to and diminish the home's overall value. The house depends on the foundation, and if you hold back on the proper development of it, the frame will surely fail.

Now, as I slip out of the practical and into the actual, let us discuss the weakness I had with self-belief (foundation) and life (frame). I had a shaky foundation from the start because, as you can recall, my self-confidence lacked influence from birth. I wobbled through life, trying to find my value. In all actuality, my inner and outer self were off balance. What I presented to the world was very different from what I concealed from it — a contradiction between how I looked and felt. All that internal grime in my head left me hopeless. It took everything in me to do anything. I would exert all of my energy trying to prevent others from noticing what was taking place on the inside of me.

To gain balance, I searched for validation apart from the condemnation that played in my head. I picked up and held fast to the unfavorable opinions of man, society's view of who and what I was to resemble, along with comparison and bad relationships. Before I knew it, the echoing of self-doubt and the ability to see greatness in everyone else but myself surfaced. My relationship with mirrors was strained because they showed me the depths of me — a person with a diminished and destroyed sense of self. I had little to no confidence, and as a result, every part of me was insecure.

See, as a person living in this world with low self-esteem, I was afraid to do anything because I felt whatever I did would result in a mistake. I was slow to speak, thinking what I said would be frowned upon. I did not trust my judgment; therefore, I would not move without explicit instructions.

Life in all its splendor created a constant threat to my self-belief, but in order to build upon that belief, I first needed to believe in me and in who I was destined to become. Look at it like this. A person cannot believe in something they do not value and cannot value something they do not love. What do I mean by that? Well, because I did not believe in me, I saw no value in me, and since all I saw was the insignificance of me, I had no reason to love me. I wanted to change how I felt about me, but to do that, I had to change what I was thinking about me too.

It was in this space that I recognized how much I disliked myself. I wanted the old me gone, and I wanted to become new (2 Corinthians 5:17). Living became too much for me to bear, but one night, after hours of crying and begging God to take my life (my usual plea), something changed. I began to think about life and found that I did not like what I had discovered. This recognition helped me understand that in order for me to be okay with who I was, I had to appreciate and value *me*, which would enable me to move comfortably within myself. Then suddenly, it dawned on me: if I wanted to get beyond this, I needed to learn to love me . . . *all of me!*

This was when I came to accept that I had a distinct relational obligation to myself to seek holistic ways of mending every broken place. It was at that moment that I began to break away from my old patterns and behaviors. I started to acknowledge, identify, accept, deal with, and finally let go of my insecurities. I did this by replacing the habits of my uncertainties with self-acceptance. I began to embrace every part of me — including but not limited to my flaws, my shortcomings, and my limitations. I studied and rehearsed how God viewed me and began telling myself that I am the design of God, so I am not a mistake. I am forgiven, I am chosen, and He exchanged His life for my own, so I am wanted; He showed me grace so that I could have the choice of salvation. I am loved, and I am His child! I not only had to rehearse these statements, but I had to accept and consume them too.

I went from begging God to take my life to asking Him for instructions on how to live it. This sudden insight allowed me to awaken from the stupor of self-doubt, giving me the courage to stop living silently behind the wall of life and start showing up for it and living it out loud! Accepting and embracing what I meant to God helped me to understand who I "really" was.

Self-awareness has now manifested and taught me that negative thoughts will form. That is something that I cannot stop; however, I can change my belief in them. Let me use an example from an earlier chapter to show you what I mean. Remember how I shared with you how debilitating it was for me to speak to someone, and they not respond with an equal level of enthusiasm? Well, I now have a new perspective on that scenario. Today, if I speak and am not greeted with the same level of enthusiasm, rather than thinking the individual does not like me, I assume that the individual did not hear me or maybe did not see me. Can you see the difference?

I had to shift my mindset. You know, change my perspective by changing the way I thought and viewed things. I became mindful of my thoughts and the rationale of how I perceived and explained what I was feeling. Doing this allowed me to feel my feelings by helping me to better understand my emotions. Understanding my emotions enabled them to arise and proved to be effective in that I could now identify and pinpoint the origin of my triggers.

Applying this renewed mindset to every aspect of my life changed how I viewed me, y'all! I gradually began to love me and soon realized that this self-love was a force that had the ability to change everything in and around my life. Loving me made it easy to be true to me, especially since I had a newfound appreciation of me.

I want to go a little deeper, and in doing so, let you know that loving me is still a bit rough to maintain at times, and because of this, it is important to understand that alongside self-love comes self-care. Self-love is when you have come to the place of loving you unapologetically, whereas self-care is taking the time to feel comfortable in your skin. Self-care is the part of self-love that involves caring for yourself.

God started dealing with me about self-care and helped me to see that it went beyond the exterior. Self-care is not bubble baths with aromatherapy candles. It is not a manicure and pedicure. It goes beyond merely getting dolled up. All of the aforementioned are self-care practices that make it easier for you to relax. Now, before I continue, what I am about to say is not for those who have it all together; this is for those who (once like me,) try to hide behind things that bring temporary satisfaction.

Self-care begins within and is an activity that focuses on your mental and emotional well-being and is only as effective as you make it. It is coming into your own and setting boundaries that block things that are not good to and for you, allowing into your space only those things that bring you peace. Listen, I begin to realize that self-care required more than care practices. It required the mindfulness to create a life that I could live with, you know, one that I did not feel the need to escape. I had to learn to view my life as meaningful instead of seeing it as meaningless. I had to detach my thoughts and emotions from the self-judgment that surfaced because of the guilt and shame of my past. This was when I truly began to understand that I was not what I lost, I was not my pain, nor was I what I thought (whether real or imagined).

I undermined my value for years but now understand that a mirror cannot judge without opinion, and since it is a new day, I miss no opportunity to look into one. With that said, let me ask you something. What are you telling yourself about you? I want to encourage you to change your perspective and to challenge you to stand boldly in acknowledging and expressing your value. I have grown to love who I am because I had to fight so hard to become! Never forget that feelings follow thoughts and that how you view yourself and the quality of your life starts and stops with what you think! The most important person I desire to know (outside of God) is ME!

Take some time to get to know you as well!

Thoughtful Considerations

What does self-love mean to you?

_____

_____

_____

_____

_____

_____

_____

_____

_____

_____

_____

_____

_____

_____

_____

_____

_____

_____

_____

_____

_____

_____

What is your definition of self-care? How do you practice it in your everyday life?

_____

_____

_____

_____

_____

_____

_____

_____

_____

_____

_____

_____

_____

_____

_____

_____

_____

_____

_____

_____

_____

_____

What do you feel the relationship is between self-love, self-worth, and self-care?

_____

_____

_____

_____

_____

_____

_____

_____

_____

_____

_____

_____

_____

_____

_____

_____

_____

_____

_____

_____

_____

_____

Lifeline

Not too long ago, my life was a complete and total mess. I was dressed up on the outside but ripped to shreds on the inside. My head was low and tilted back with my mouth nearing water level; I was unable to control my involuntary arm movements and eventually found myself floating face down, gasping for life, drowning — silently.

I was unfamiliar with this body of water. Looking out into the unknown and not being able to focus distorted my sense of direction. I was unable to determine what I needed to survive. It was like Déjà vu, waiting and hoping for someone, someday, to come to my rescue. Escaping this situation was imperative, a matter of life and death. I needed strength because I had none. I needed someone or something on which I could depend. I needed an anchored line thrown to me as a display of support to ease my distress. I needed a safety measure to protect and save me.

For me, a lifeline is someone I can always depend on to help me in hard times. It [lifeline] is someone who lets me be me (no matter what). Someone who encourages me to keep going even when I am out of breath, girt, or will. Someone who believes in me even when I do not believe in myself. Someone who sees me as flawed, yet loves me just as I am. Someone who cares enough to tell me (in love) what is right, even if doing so will bruise my feelings. Someone who will talk to me tirelessly day in and day out until what I feel dissipates. Someone who enjoys and appreciates the laughing, cut up part of me. Someone who has seen me cry repeatedly and think it not strange. Someone who lets me fuss and still loves me just the same. Someone who promises not to tell my secrets but tells them anyway because my life is more important than years of not speaking.

In essence, a lifeline to me represents all of God's gifts to me. Gifts known as family and friends who were all strategically placed in my life during certain times of life. Each of whom have played a vital role in preventing me from drowning.

The need for this was great in my life, and although I was alive, I could not help but notice how I had come very close to the edge many times. I certainly was not operating at my fullest capacity and found comfort in watching everything I was, crumble to inexact pieces. However, God knew me before I was formed in my mother's womb and knew exactly what life would bring. Even though there has been a lot of uncertainty along this journey, God has always been right there. He has been faithful and has shown me the power of His might. It was not until I could clearly see my way that I was able to know and understand Him in His fullness. I promise you, He is the source of my existence. I mean that literally. Of course, I am here because of Him, but more specifically, He is my fuel. He is what keeps me going. In Him is where my hope resides. I would be remiss if I did not endlessly thank Him for being who He is in my life — He knew I would need Him!

To look around now and see my current posture as compared to how I was positioned years ago is mind-blowing! I do not know how I am standing or even how I am here except had it not been for God, my family, and friends. There were many times during this journey that I just wanted to walk out on life, desiring to live no more. I was tired of fighting. I had to fight for my name, my identity, my sanity, my character, my space, and my life. However, I had to go through my life "then" in order to experience my life "now" — a life that has made me who I am today. To know me is to love me!

LIFELINES

The Winslow family: my brother-in-law, sister, and nephews, gosh . . . where do I begin? I have so much to say — there are not enough hours in the day. I appreciate and love you so very much! I was blessed with the best family in the world! You all never gave up on me, even when I was making bad life decisions. You all have been an outstanding support system. Through you, I have seen and been taught strength and courage, and I would not be where I am today had it not been for your guidance.

Thank you from the bottom of my heart for giving me a second chance at getting this life thing right! You did not have to be there for me, but you were and without hesitation. Thank you for making such a tremendous impact in and on my life. Thank you for being such great role models. Thank you for showing me the love that is genuinely shared between a husband, wife, and family. Thank you for your never-ending and unconditional love. Thank you for being my calm when I needed it most. My gratitude is immeasurable, and I love you guys more than you will ever know.

I want to thank all of my lifelines who have been mentioned throughout the book for praying for me and with me, for the words of life spoken over me, for understanding me, for remaining YOU while letting me be ME, and most of all, for never giving up on me. I love you all! Here is to a lifetime of family and friendship! I now see that *change* was my exodus.

Thoughtful Considerations

How did your lifeline keep you from drowning?

_____

_____

_____

_____

_____

_____

_____

_____

_____

_____

_____

_____

_____

_____

_____

_____

_____

_____

_____

_____

_____

_____

_____

_____

_____

Have you ever found yourself drowning in a situation? If so, describe how that situation lead you to fulfilling your purpose.

_____

_____

_____

_____

_____

_____

_____

_____

_____

_____

_____

_____

_____

_____

_____

_____

_____

_____

_____

_____

_____

_____

_____

_____

_____

In fulfilling your purpose, what steps can you take now to assure you remain on task?

_____

_____

_____

_____

_____

_____

_____

_____

_____

_____

_____

_____

_____

_____

_____

_____

_____

_____

_____

_____

_____

_____

_____

The Joy in Birthing Pain

Many of us have experienced pain, whether physical, emotional, or both, so there is no need to describe what it is like. However, I cannot attest to one pain, which is the pain of childbirth, because although I have been pregnant, I did not make it to full term. My memories of being pregnant are associated with a relentless clash of uncertainty, fear, happiness, nervousness, love, pain, and joy. I would crave strawberry Pop Tarts coated in butter, had a strong sensitivity to almost every smell known to man, and morning sickness showed me no mercy!

That is as far as it went for me; however, I know women who have had children, and while their experiences differ, there was one common denominator — PAIN!

In pregnancy, a mother experiences pains that denote different stages of the baby's development. The development of the baby is made visible by the expansion of the mother's belly, which then undergoes a discomforting stretch, which occurs to make room for the anticipated push surrounding the joy of birthing new life. Pushing new life is uncomfortable because it forces you to confront that which is causing you pain.

My actual going through pain was anything but joyous — the birthing of brokenness, irrelevance, hurt, rejection, abandonment, disappointment, fear, resentment, sadness, anger, physical, sexual, and mental abuse subdued me. I became numb, dying inside. Yet, walking through and not around my pain helped me see that I had to embrace it [pain] to experience joy.

Let's go back to Proverbs 13:12, and this time quote the entire Scripture: "Hope deferred makes the heart sick, but a longing fulfilled is a tree of life." Do you know what this tells me? That the hope that makes the heart sick is the same hope that makes the heart well. For a long time, even with a heavy heart and tears in my eyes, I walked around my pain, meaning I avoided it but quickly discovered that waiting for the pain to pass did not produce healing. Healing came when I allowed myself to confront and feel the pain. It is how I learned to look beyond it, especially knowing it was associated with what was being created in me.

Facing my pain changed me and eventually shaped me into a more well-developed, evolved, complete, healed, and whole person.

Understanding "The Joy in Birthing Pain" is knowing that joy not only pushed me through the pain; it was also the award that awaited me after having endured it. One of the greatest joys that manifested out of my pain was getting back to God and arriving at a place where I am holding His promises in my hand. The night of my weeping lasted for what seemed to be forever, but the morning did come.

And David slew Goliath!

About the Author

Tammy Boone, better known as Tammy Raé, uplifts and inspires the lives of women everywhere through her speaking, coaching, writing, mentoring, and community involvement.

It is in this space that she helps transform lives as she shares her formal and experiential experiences with humility, transparency, vulnerability, and conviction.

Tammy Raé has a passion for reaching women and teaching them how to press beyond their stuck and and believes if she can do it, anybody can!

Connect with Tammy Raé to schedule coaching or mentoring sessions, or to book her for speaking engagements, by reaching out to her at www.tammyrae.net

www.ingramcontent.com/pod-product-compliance
Lightning Source LLC
Chambersburg PA
CBHW060008050426
42448CB00028B/1945